Book of Days

Also by David Lindley

POETRY
The Night Outside
Five, Seven, Five
Something & Nothing: Selected Poems

PROSE
Ideas of Order
The Freedom to Be Tragic

BOOK OF DAYS

David Lindley

Verborum Editions

© David Lindley 2014

First published 2014 by Verborum Editions

Verborum Editions
5 Lauds Road
Crick
Northamptonshire
England
NN6 7TJ

www.verborumeditions.com

Set in Janson

Book designed by Sarah Rock

Cover photo:
'Rust' by James Lindley

978-1-907100-03-1

for Caron

The year 1993

Thank you for all the days

JANUARY

Farmyard ducks splash homeward.
At the ford, evening
and a lovers' meeting.

•

In fields white with frost
the mole works out of sight.
Dark humps of earth.

•

The moon retreats and tides
and passions of the blood
are in abeyance.

•

First day
setting off
in new shoes.

•

Turning over brown
leaves of the past.
What was it
I wanted to know?

•

Unfinished stepping stones
tempt us farther out
nervously like bathers.

BOOK OF DAYS

So long apart
no words to say
that can't be said
in loving glances.

•

Surprised in the shower
by a fresh salmon.
Two mouths fall open.

•

Tonight we thought again
of Monet's house hidden
behind yellow flowers.

•

Rain endlessly falling.
Sitting quietly
doing nothing.

•

For the first time
she danced a little.
We read that Nureyev
had died.

•

Flowers, a chapel.
It enters my body
the breath of the saintly corpse.

In the heart
a soft release of wings.
Gulls fly up
from the flooded field.

•

Sun after the rain.
Geese fly in to the river
arriving feet first.

•

This is not after all
such simple fare –
potatoes dug in Egypt.

•

Eating pheasant in red wine
thinking of one who flew
from flood to flood.

•

Intimations of the spring –
flowers in bud
among new graves
flight of crows.

•

After the long journey
even in sleep
I keep travelling.

After many weeks
the apprentice bohemian
made her first boots.

•

Something to celebrate –
children learn to cut pasta
and put on their shoes.

•

Early morning ploughing.
Against the grey sky
a tumult of white wings.

•

These cries
would be wonderful to hear.
The silence of the house next door.

•

A winding river
the road descending
in the rain
a red barn.

•

A night of storms.
Unbroken by the wind
the first snowdrops
of the spring.

Não é um dia por os sonhos.
Está frio em Londres
está frio em Lisboa.

•

This is the worst of fates
to have died young
and not imagined anything.

•

Pencilled lines mark
where they will appear.
Bright Chinese lanterns.

•

These are not my memories
but the dead still feud
and invade my dreams.

•

A bare brown field
seen through the hedge.
A lone pheasant.

•

On the hill saplings
planted in neat rows,
a memorial forest.

Crows
above the village houses
arguing
where and how to live.

FEBRUARY

Scattered feathers,
Monday morning birds
casually whistling.

•

The news is ominous
but does not mention
lapwing blackening the sky.

•

Thoughts enclose you
like a building without windows.
Outside is somewhere.

•

The days are such
that we may fail to count them
forgetting the rule
to let nothing get by.
If the mind must be ensnared
let it not be by dullness.
There must be no escaping
this net of sense and experience.

•

People idly gossip.
The world manages somehow
without effort.

Kestrel hugged
to itself waiting
for the mist to clear.

•

Daffodils forced into spring
flower pale and exhausted
atop their stems.

•

Side by side their silver heads
bob in adjacent kitchens
making lunch.

•

Plough turning earth
black lapwing black
falling rising white.

•

He lies asleep
lights out
so much invention
arising from the heart.

•

Wine bottles rattling
in the back but no servant
to lift me on the cart.

The promise of spring
is enough.
She puts aside
the glass of wine.

•

Pigs in the mist
grubbing in the fields
outside their tin houses.

•

Noisy argument
outside my door.
A hundred sparrows in the tree.

•

A crowded train
to Wolverhampton
talking of Paris
and painters.

•

Hair combs just like hers
abandoned on the table
her door left open.

•

Revealed behind the wallpaper
Etruscan landscapes
with cypresses.

Rosemary arrives
with a huge rose tree
to cover the potting shed.

•

The sun shone sometimes
it was the sun sometimes
the painted yellow door.

•

Held in the hand
the bamboo balance
weighs out measures
of Chinese roots.

•

She calculates on the abacus
the characters
for root and bark.

•

Strong medshun good for you
this prescribing make the blood
go round like this.

•

When you complained
of cold feet did you mean
also this fear of each day?

Ancient cures are best.
See how the broken earth
serves the squabble of gulls.

•

Lapwing rise
exciting the air
between you
and your horizon.

•

Today the lapwing rest
content at their feasting
hidden in the grass.

•

Already the crows
are struggling with sticks
too big for them
against the wind.

•

Flurry of snow and wood smoke.
Someone says pass
another log for the fire.

MARCH

BOOK OF DAYS

Cypress hung with snow
its branches green and white.
A wren darts in and out.

•

The snow gone they venture out
from under the hedgerows,
leaves blown by the wind.

•

The east wind
finds its way in
to where I sit
by the empty grate.

•

In the morning
gypsies were there.
Tethered goats and ponies.

•

How came this northern painter
to stumble upon
Monet's gingerbread house?

•

If your art is true
the hills themselves
will come round
to your point of view.

BOOK OF DAYS

Finches crowd into the hedges
madly singing
among the budding branches.

•

The sun hangs in the sky
like a festive balloon.
Shirts join hands and dance.

•

Spring sowing yields
flocks of wood pigeons
grey patches in the fields.

•

Two by two
hurrying to work
two by two
swans flying overhead.

•

Sowing by lamplight.
In the beam of tractors
white moths.

•

Balloon descending
the way we too
came down once
behind the hill.

People in overcoats
surprised by the sun
and the sudden blue sky.

•

With a beakful
of wet leaves
the crow tries to finish
its latticework nest.

•

Looking for spring
I end up with poems
instead of daffodils.

•

Over the stone bridge
down the stone alleyway
still stands the stone angel.

•

To fox and badger
the field offers up
yellow primroses.

•

The house is filled with flowers
now she is here
in her new yellow dress.

The men from the village
are planting alder and oak
with new spades.

•

They are here at last
young leaves
weeping on the willow.

•

New buds hard as fists.
In the grass
last year's chestnuts.

•

Cold morning.
A bee tentatively
exploring primroses.

APRIL

White
plastic bags tied
to sticks
in the green fields
blowing like yachts
in rough seas.

•

The earth bears
everything
even your sadness.

•

Each spring
when the hawthorn
blossoms
we both remember
the same white
hedged lane.

•

Stone pillars
where the bridge
will be built
are like classical
columns
already ruins.

If I just said
yes to Ma Zhe
tomorrow
I could easily be
in Shen Yang.

•

In the wind and rain
I stop to buy fresh fish.
My loose change
smells of the sea.

•

Where would the blackbird
sit if we cut off
the broken branch of the plum?

•

Spring's first arrivals
were always bluebells
brought home
from the deep woods.

•

You hurry home
to match the landscape
to your box of colours.

BOOK OF DAYS

A field of headstones
encircled by a stone wall
in a landscape of stones.

•

A Jack Russell
in the cab of a roller
keeps one eye
on the road works.
Tea steams
behind the sun.

•

Last year's plums
dried hard
on the branch
wrinkled
as a pharaoh's testicles.

•

Firmly under her hand
side by side appear
fields and trees and the sun.

•

School begins
but still she sits by the pond
finishing her book.

BOOK OF DAYS

Rapeseed in flower
slashes of yellow
behind the red barn.

•

The pheasants are skittish
risking their long tails
over the hawthorn hedges.

•

White feathers, white petals
blown on the wind
vanishing like spring snow.

•

A yellow field
under a grey sky.
A white goose flies up.

•

Cows moo behind the house
bees buzz around the front door
painted bright yellow.

•

I love footnotes
one that says
for Byzantine silk export rules
see

Under the moon
all night the cows chew
elegant white grasses.

•

The lanes are so full of leaf
only the sky shows through.
A heron.

•

Take the camera
go to China
capture once
the receding landscape.

•

The wood edged in white,
sea foam floating
on the horizon.

MAY

We are used to planes
overhead but not this fast
arrowhead of pigeons.

•

Today we fixed everything.
The sun shines
over our green parasol.

•

Cockerels by the old gatehouse.
In the churchyard lambs
bleat among the headstones.

•

An old toothbrush
will do for this kind of tree.
The Chinese used dried grass.

•

On the green
under the candelabras
of chestnut trees
thrushes tethered
to worms.

You were already home
your yellow dress
laid out neatly on the bed.

•

An apple pie
bright with sugar
still hot when
it went into the box.

•

Something made her smile
at this crab
that used to scuttle under the sea.

•

Done.
Dusted.
Scones for tea.

•

What are you anxious about –
skies, distances, absence,
this warm body?

•

All three are here now –
house martins, wisteria
under the eaves, spring.

A boy is digging a hole
to get to the other side
of the world.
Here we are.

•

Charles Bridge.
The wide open spaces
filled with the trinkets of freedom.

•

We kneel and pray
together and ask
how we are to turn
bread into one body.

•

Now we are thirty
she said and we have won
– this emptiness.

•

The Dies Irae eventually tires
and you pick up a book
to pass the time.

•

We are apart
and she is alone
closed like a pink flower
in the night.

We drink the last
of the wine
and head for the vineyard.

•

What is this we take
to barter with?
The head of Bartolomeu Dias.

•

All week we have been discussing
strategy. Sun Tzu
settles it all at once.

•

The cuckoo
has been calling
us since dawn
but we will not get up.

•

One day the sun will shine
one day we will have paid
for this costly fish.

•

We eat the fresh river
fish and then
go in search of an umbrella.

Rain.
From the mouth of the cave
we watch the sea
break on the rocks.

•

The dried codfish was excellent.
After dinner we browsed
through three volumes of Bocage.

•

Cowbells
in the orange grove.
We pick more
than we can carry.

•

A house abandoned
under the olive trees.
This is the room
where the donkey lived.

•

A nest of kittens
feasts on yesterday's sardines.
Ants pick the bones clean.

•

Outside under the fountain
the great white book
lies open and unread.

JUNE

When the cathedral bell
sounds the gypsy girl
sits down promptly
to unwrap her lunch.

•

These fish are good fresh
these dried in the net
the flies have found
are thrown back.

•

The old lady in black
crosses the tracks
and bends for the child's kiss.

•

Upstairs the child's
crying descends
like grey drizzle.

•

After days of endless rain
I pick three flowers
for your posy.

•

The flowers draw you aside
impatiently seeking
their completeness.

THE RETURN

The white plastic reflection
distorted under the surface
is no trapped wing
or imprisoned soul

the still water seems to deny
the imagination flat
mundane incapable
of supporting a miracle

yet while we look away
out of the desultory floating
weed the cheeping moorhen
recreates itself

the swans are followed
by grey remembrances
of themselves
and out of sight

from mud and slime
the caught wing rises
like a thought
beginning its brilliant flight.

The crowd goes by
unsatisfied. Soon enough
I'll have nothing to say.

•

Blue field like the sky
below the yellow field
above the yellow sun
in the blue sky.

•

Clay faces
moulded by
fingers following
remembered contours.

•

Frightened mole
behind a fallen leaf.
Tears.

•

My wisest words
after all were his
and he got them
from his brother.

•

Someone waist high
in the blue fields at evening
just looking.

'I will go to my village
and become a shaman
and eat fish.' Xingu Indian

•

Boats moored
among geraniums.
Geese waiting
for the lock to open.

•

Each day new colours
flower in the garden.
No one knows what the plan is.

•

We have no way of knowing
only a way of seeing
again and again.

•

The sea has invaded the fields.
Over the hedgerows
waves of blue flax.

•

Glints of sun on brass
and silver. Children
at their rowdy band practice.

JULY

Words are a betrayal
but these fields and hills
cannot betray you.

•

Now you have more work
than ever recreating
yourself each day.

•

Love breaks the cold heart
that knows itself watching
beyond the reach of passion.

•

In the church
a bass voice rumbles
among the stone pillars.

•

Between us hands and eyes
create blue shadows
among the green foliage.

•

The mind is slow
to recognise the world.
The giant rabbit
looks down from on high.

I dream. I am not.
I cease to dream.
A volume of words
put away.

•

When the page was blank
no one thought suddenly
a flower will appear.

•

Who cast down these stones?
The same who in the beginning
said God is great.

•

Where are Christ's bones?
Sterne's are here, this jest.
The sun through Christ's nailed arms.

•

How can you not
be angry with them?
Turn to something that matters.

•

A hedgehog by the gate.
No. Moss
tossed from the gutter
by sparrows.

My head needs time
to get used to the falling
price of Chablis.

•

These colours and perfumes
are essences somehow
walked past and missed.

•

A word to a friend
can transform hard winter
into summer's ease.

•

Through the frosted glass
there are only colours.
So whose garden is this?

•

To master this movement
of hand or brush
first we must master our breath.

•

The blackbird has no plan
but always knows
where the cherries are.

BOOK OF DAYS

The cloud doesn't shift
hanging oppressively
like damp laundry.

•

The houses are strange
no one will tell her
what these plants are for
and the cloud will not break.

•

A long journey back
from nowhere in bad weather
and no tales to tell.

•

The rooms themselves
hold a tragedy
narrow stairs
closed blinds
half light.

•

They eat here
now they're retired
roast beef
liebfraumilch
the rain
the garden.

The rain falls endlessly.
I look out through the beaded pane
like one exiled.

•

After years apart
now she is dying
she remembers the little girl.

•

These are bitter torrents.
All night the rain
cuts off yesterday and tomorrow.

•

A lone snail hangs arrogantly
from the last leaf
of the dahlia.

•

Thunder flies speckle the air.
We are all waiting
for the rain.

•

Two mates in a hired van
fresh fish from this morning's trawler.
Perhaps.

She waves.
Already
I had forgotten
how small she is
in my arms.

•

Watering slow growing
mountain plants
has a way of centring
a life by osmosis.

AUGUST

Thousands read but
no one remembers.
Water shatters like falling glass.

•

The barn owl's white face turns
alert to nothing more
than men at the bar.

•

Hay wagons roll by.
Hedgehog rolls into a ball
all prickles, snout out.

•

The sunflowers are whispering again
heads nodding together
unaware of their fall.

•

The old learning is put away.
There are new things to know
up on the hills.

•

Saved from the fire
a woman walks with her companion,
man, beast or bird.

Peacock butterflies
are everywhere
on coffee cups and newspapers.

•

After a brief conversation
swallows move on
across the lichened roofs.

•

Chickens cross the road
the wind blows and the first
chestnuts begin to fall.

•

Ungainly on their feet
grey cygnets show off
their white swans' wings.

•

The war is over.
The colours and shapes
of things observed are saved.

•

The dark day fades
from memory and the bright
evening welcomes you home.

Today the house is full of flowers.
Outside the window
a bright red poppy.

•

Leaves already yellowing
in the hedgerows
among berries yet to ripen.

•

The gates stand open
to receive the harvest.
Swifts skim fields
stacked with gold.

•

We are crowds without power
moved by the words
of Antony to witness.

•

The field are too full
of the golden grain
and the flax is as fair
as a spinning maid.
They overflow
like hoarded treasure
or hearts that have burst
with a golden pleasure.

How fortunate the fields are
cropped to golden squares
to be so dry and August-like
under a blue sky.

•

The red house
on the green hill
says it must be so.

•

The plough scrawls
verses across
the earth.

•

At some word
I missed the swallows
fly up from the eaves.

•

All week the giant
combines have worked
in a golden haze.

•

Each evening men
follow the trucks of grain
with gold dust on their boots.

By Cleobury steeple
we study ritual masks
and the mosques of Mali.

•

Coming down from the ridge
we stop to listen
to the bent heads of barley.

•

The sheep are marked
for slaughter each unaware
of what has been written.

•

They return to bleach white
the long dry furrows.
Gulls following the plough.

•

I waft it away without thought
the dragonfly of a moment
come to rest on my nose.

SEPTEMBER

Men are painting the school railings
a bright green
painting them
memory by memory.

•

The flowers I bought stink.
Too many memories
and too much work to be done.

•

At last we break through.
Where all was still and listless
a continent comes into view.

•

Tipped this way the head
falls to one side
and eyes close
and the image changes
from proud prince
to crucified Christ
our divine sorrow.

•

Rain fills the pond
under the rainbow
snails drowned in a pool.

BOOK OF DAYS

A dream of discovery
dialogues in the dark
runic words in an old book.

•

The stone marks
where the dead
must lie and no one
now remembers the duty
that called them here.

•

The church door stands open
but no one enters
for the celestial banquet.

•

The bells ring out.
Love and death
have been here
and still they call you.

•

Oxfordshire
shriven fields
birdsong
and a looming sky.

•

Young oak laden
with green acorns.
I might sit here
and wait a month.

In motley
red trousers
green shoes
black hat
against the rain
intoxicated
by the turning leaves
he had become
shaman
spirit of autumn
touching every tree
one after the other
dressed
in motley.

•

The windows will open
at your head and ankle
and morning will suddenly
grow loud with singing.

•

Close to the earth seems best
bedding in new plants
with a handful of dust.

•

This
is the taste
of dry dust.

The roads have changed
my memory is like an old map
and in my dream
I follow invisible paths.

•

Moon in a blue afternoon
in the eye of a cloud a balloon
and the little dog laughed.

•

Where swallows dipped
among the sheaves lapwing
return to the bare earth.

•

The words we are used to
autumn moon rain
will not serve without
the thought we have forgotten.

HIEROGLYPH

Time hangs like round fruit
on the tree
the dove denotes
the space it flies through.

They call it bookish learning
who don't know these ghosts
and their dark recollections.

•

Now I've found the passage
I need it's too late
I have to leave.

•

Two crows in conversation
on a dead stump watch
the clouds darkening the sky.

•

The road ends at the river.
An old tug will ferry you
across through the driftwood.

•

A long standoff.
Once a paw is raised
samurai puss
it can't be revoked.

OCTOBER

The boy leans back his head.
Raindrops from the eaves
above – infinite space.

•

Asleep in the afternoon.
Chinese characters marching
together do not make a poem.

•

A week of rain.
Apples have rolled
onto the roof
yellow and red.

•

In the evening light
starlings gather on wires
like abacus beads.

•

Everywhere an over-ripeness
a prowling cat distracted
by leaves
birds on every branch
calling alarm
sudden fall of apples.

Half the sky is black
with the coming storm
(Payne's grey she says)
the leaves painted gold.

•

Yellow leaves cover the path.
In the green wheelbarrow
red apples.

•

The rainbow ends somewhere
here by the bell tower
among fallen gravestones.

•

Pale autumn leaves
irresolute in flight
like summer butterflies.

•

This is all a poet achieves
windfall fruit
some other leaves.

•

Apples hang like red
and gold lanterns
extinguished now
by night and rain.

Reminiscing.
1968.
Lost causes
forgotten names.

•

Parents lament
but children enjoy
floating along flooded streets.

•

That evil star
not far above the horizon
an emerald in the frost.

•

The frost takes us by surprise.
We light the fire
with last year's logs.

•

Moorhens dart in and out
of the floating leaves.
The swans have flown.

•

The fields assume
the reserved idiom of winter.
The hedgerows celebrate
with bright clusters of holly.

We wake to find the leaves
that filtered the light
are gone the branches
covered with frost
and the air white.

•

The grass is cut
for the last time
withered plants
are piled up in heaps.

•

Children gather fallen leaves
in one big heap under the tree
in the playground for no reason
they can explain except the need
to gather in their arms some
reckoning of the abundant season.

•

If the Empress of China
were to pass by
she would walk and look like this.

•

Small brown leaves are blown
from tree to tree –
occasionally one is a wren.

Days are shortened
by decree and ceremonials
of the past dissolved.

•

If you are afraid
it is only some old corpuscles
complaining on their way.

•

In the house
pages are turning.
Outside leaves
are rolling over and over.

•

While you were working
the apple blossom fell one day
in a shower and apples
grew into their colours.
Here they are in a bowl.

•

They all have a way of seeing,
few words but a good eye
for what satisfies or delights.

•

Both arms raised
in some sort of invocation
a closed fist, an open palm
a spirit flowing through arteries.

Everything that moves
may be something else
a blown leaf, tremor
of grass, a mouse, wren.

NOVEMBER

Happy birthday to you
is still in copyright
and royalties are due
until 1996
(but this line is free).

•

The garden is abandoned
apples are overripe
and Adam with his flute
recalls a forgotten tune.

•

More satisfying than summer
Mapplethorpe's cloudless flowers
ablaze.

•

The wood is thin
and full of light
and a wind
that blows through it.

•

Everything seems
to have lost its will.
Crows and leaves
blown by the wind.

BOOK OF DAYS

A dove alights
on the bare tree.
Someone in a drowned world
waits for a sign from me.

•

The crows are around somewhere
but not in their nests
wrecked by wind and rain.

•

If you move to a new place
a stone's throw away
the stone you throw
might put stars to flight,
stir camels, elephants
or gee-up passing reindeer.

•

The roads are all byways
tracks and muddy lanes
there is no direct route.
Two or three valleys
get in the way
of being anywhere else.
A thin line snakes
over the hill for travellers
and the discontented.

The rain is relentless.
Dreaming head bowed
through the broken streets
towards a lighted window.

•

O the west wind
the fallen November leaves
passing without ceremony.

•

The future is immense
and irrevocable.
Just sign here
and wait.

•

Paintings lie around
waiting to be hung
in another place
yet to be journeyed to.

•

The car radio is fixed at last.
Mozart. Unexpectedly
the swans return.

•

Farms float away
from their ditches
all doors and paths
lead to the water's edge.

BOOK OF DAYS

These two arm in arm
pottering along cold streets
looking for Rembrandt.

•

The city in winter
tramlines through
the thin wood
a cold wait.

•

The fields are frozen.
When darkness comes
all along the horizon
glasshouses ablaze with light.

•

In the first flurry of snow
blackbirds scurry low
under white branches.

•

Birds chatter somewhere
in the fog
in the garden
no footprints in the snow.

•

Solitary pheasant
in the snow
pecking pecking pecking.

BOOK OF DAYS

We must endure
both these hard things
our own integrity
and those who trespass.

•

They are up from the valleys
to look and to wish
sharing small change
for the bus fare home.

•

In the wind birds
scattered like yellowed leaves.
In a bowl bright
oranges with green wings.

•

Work drives away death?
It just waits for the inevitable
lapse of concentration.

•

The moon
a trickster
among the clouds.
When did I last
look up
when, when?

DECEMBER

Until the mist clears
the church and its steeple
are suspended between
earth and sky.

•

Lapwing rising
from the fields
cross the frame
of the window
and everyone
stops to look.

•

A mother to a sullen child:
We have too much to do
for you to enjoy yourself
battling alien invaders.

•

Furthermore
this is a nice weekend
and I am wishing
it does not end.

•

Just when I think
I might go straight
someone reminds me
how important it is
to be weird.

And there is sustenance
in an idea
a passionate principle
despite bad practice.

•

An old inn
by the lichgate
fresh fish
brought over the moors
in the storm.

•

Old friends out of place
frayed shabby books
on strange shelves.

•

What are the crows
doing up there
scratching around in the wind?

•

Robins are puffed out
against the cold
well fed cats stroll by.

•

As you leave
you glance at the empty page.
In time everything will be fulfilled.

Even in the dark
when you arrive
the signpost to the sea
changes everything.

•

In the morning
the floods had burst
over the black fields
and turned to ice.

•

Away from the crowds
I push open the church door.
Instead of silence
the choir rehearsing.

•

Enough of this
alone in the dark
listening to the rain
thinking
of her warm knees.

•

He ambles through the day
a character in a story
his mind somewhere else
looking down on darkness.

Games for the children.
Then I remember
how old they are
and go back for the beer.

•

While bishops say they have their doubt
we sing and praise
these wondrous days
then Miss Team Vicar sees us out.

•

Few could tell or care
this is the Feast of Thomas the Apostle
or sing your health or drink your wassail
bless your cow or mare.

•

This stuff costs ten pounds a bottle.
What kind is it?
Ten past three he said
studying his watch.
It was quarter to five.

•

After many years
we speak hesitantly
of the past wondering
if there is something
to forgive.

Christmas Eve.
Leopards and crocodiles
stalk through the holly.
Africans with parasols
leave the wooden church.

•

The fairytale turret
where she listened
and dreamed
is now a lumber room.

•

In a white house
facing north across
the frozen river
she thinks of the old
southern capital
the cloisters
and water meadows.

•

We pack bright coloured things.
We are getting wings
and intend to fly south for the winter.

•

A sheep caught on the wire.
Those who are free graze
indifferent to one
whose fate is to suffer.

So much of scholarly importance
has been exhausted.
These early tulips
forced into spring
bow their heads
defeated.

•

The present moment
ebbs away colourless.
The drone of engines passing.

•

The bright bird of morning
that lifts us above the clouds
insists the moment
is a nameless bird of paradise
a scent that reaches us
before the flower opens.

www.ingramcontent.com/pod-product-compliance
Lightning Source LLC
Chambersburg PA
CBHW051707040426
42446CB00008B/765